CLEAVE

Also by Pamela Johnson Parker

A Walk Through the Memory Palace (2009) —Phoenicia
Other Four-Letter Words (2009) —Finishing Line

CLEAVE

Poems by Pamela Johnson Parker

Winner of the 2017 Trio Award

Parker, Pamela Johnson
1st edition.

ISBN: 978-0-9965864-8-1
Library of Congress Control Number: 2017955108

Interior Layout & Cover Design by Lea C. Deschenes
Cover Artwork by Carrie Ann Baade
Editing by Joanna Penn Cooper & Tayve Neese

Printed in Tennessee, USA
Trio House Press, Inc.
Ponte Vedra Beach, FL

To contact the author, send an email to tayveneese@gmail.com.

for Harvey

TABLE OF CONTENTS

TO CLING TO

TO CLEAVE

Who is she who, coming up from the desert,
does cleave to her beloved, who awakened her?

—Song of Songs 8:5

Still Life with Wicker

Who reads these leaves, these
Leavings? Spoon on its side, plow
Blade half-buried in

The teabag's furrow?
My doing, my undoing?
Dead honeybee caught

In the daylily's
Throat? Periphrasis of the
Copperhead? Ghost of

Its just-shed skin, cast off
On the porch? You? Who promised
Cleave: *cling to, divide?*

TO DIVIDE

First Person Plural, First Person Singular

"A single line, at the bottom of a page, leaves too much space."
—Printer's Handbook

I.

I was never interested in falling, as you
Told me you had fallen, *head over heels,*

I was interested in *heels over head,*
My legs straight up, twin columns against your

Shoulders and you like Samson between them.
Veux-tu m'epouser? you'd ask, and that

Seventh time I answered, smiling, open-
Mouthed. Oh, I remember the chill of that

April day, the heat from your body caught
In your black cashmere sweater as you draped it

Carefully over my shoulders, and I
Remember that looking blinded me, that

Talking deafened me, that kissing muted
Me. I remember gesture, remember intent,

Remember intensity, remember mornings
When the tables were turned, when we over-

Turned the table, each day a lattice for
Us to twine upon like morning glories, open,
Closed and open according to the light.

II.

I see the light gone from your green eyes, I
Feel the cold of your hand, much colder, I
Think, than the chill of the anodized table I

Find you lying on; I'm aware that I
Am thinking *this is not you, this is not, I
Don't believe it.* Beloved, once I

Waited for you in the lake, breathless, I
Opened there in the water for you, I
Was origami unfolding, oh I

Was a paper flower dissolving, I
Felt your legs scissor me, heard you gasp I
Was so warm, and I was the lake and I

Was the water and then I was, I
Was, wasn't I, anything—wasn't I
Something, and I was flesh of your flesh, I

Was bone of your bone, I was one of two, I
Was singular, wasn't single. As I
Linger here, no arms to hold me as I

Shiver except my own, I am *tower,* I
Am *obelisk, obituary;* I
Am *survived by,* I am *loving wife,* I

Am *Beloved,* first person singular, I
Am poor typography, *widow,* I, I

I.

Aubade: Thrift Store Sidewalk Sestina

Here these clothes are

               somebody's, nobody's

Not really bodies but

               slipcovers in sunlight

Streaking, fading, rows

               upon rows of secondhand

Jackets, trousers, cashmeres

               heady with the scent

Of camphor, cedar, sachet; redolent

               of rooms where no silver

Wool-mad pair of mating

               moths could ever last.

Now we finger through them:

               satins, silks, this shoe last

Fastened with grosgrain;

               wonder whose bodies

These velvets once shadowed,

               who wore this silver

Sheath, shimmering thin—

               it must have clung as if light

Were skin's own halo;

               ponder what lover, sent

Packing, forgot this or that,

               whose whimsies went second-hand

Whose spring clean this was,

               sweeping clean as the second hand

Of a watch sweeps, sweeps

               past the hours. Last

Night we were lovers,

surfeited with the scent

Of sex, salt and olives;

our bodies were bodies

Of water—how we spilled,

pooled, emptied; moonlight

Maddened us, gave us context,

texture, printed us silver,

Argent photogravures. Morning

now, and we offer silver

Instead of ourselves, hiding

and seeking among secondhand

Garments. Lingerie, lace, batiste…

"Isn't this wonderfully light-

Weight?" you say. (You said

I was wonderful, last

Evening). A breeze riffles through

scarves, silk sashes. Busybodies,

How the empty dresses gossip,

and how the scent

Of someone's perfume

wafts toward us. *My Sin*'s sent

Skyward from shantung;

Obsession, from silver

Ascots, pale gray gloves. Remember

last evening, our profligate bodies

Pewter? Today, September

light dazzles damask. "One second, hand

Me that," you say. "I want this

and this." Last night I wanted, last

Night I was wanted; today I

want nothing, want to travel light,

Today I want no colors here, not
                              even the sun's, for daylight
Does no favors for old cloth, new
                              lovers; daylight should be sent
For cycles—buds, blossoms, seeds;
                              whatever's meant to last
Beyond the fall, which is too fast
                              upon us. Today I want only silver
The oh-so-opulent mercury
                              of mirrors reflecting, hand-
Glass giving back
                              to me only our bodies,

        Bodies, numinous last night, now only imagined,

        But last night sent silver, silver, lit

        By the light of the second-hand sun.

ART THROUGH THE AGES: BOTTICELLI

Thirty-two roses,
> Pink ones, to our first bed you
>> Brought, scattering them

Over the deep teal
> Percale (*Ultramarine means*
>> *Beyond the sea,* you

Told me) —but never
> Told me why. For 23
>> Years I'd ask you:

Teeth in the jawbone?
> *The freezing point of water?*
>> *Beethoven's entire*

Sonata series?
> *The waist of your Levis when*
>> *We were first wed?*

Only your half-smile
> For an answer. Until this
>> Morning, sifting through

The thicket of your
> Books, one opens to petals
>> Pressed against *The Birth*

Of Venus—roses
> Drifting across the skyscape,
>> Across the seascape,

Across the landscape
　　　Of her body, persuading
　　　　　The eye to focus

On undulation—
　　　Not the unnatural length
　　　　　Of her neck, and not

The steep precipice
　　　Of her ivory shoulders,
　　　　　And not the hinge of

Her arm against the
　　　Doorway of her body, the
　　　　　Precarity of

Balance that she couldn't
　　　Possibly keep on the umbo
　　　　　Of that scallop.

ORNITHOLOGY: WILD CANARIES

Daze of late August,
      When thimbles of coneflower
            Seeds stand out in stark

Relief, as the hot
      Pink petals droop, drop away,
            How he and she break

Off from their flock,
      In an undulation (their
            Flight reminiscent

Of a holy roller
      Coaster) and then begin to
            Nest. Grasses, needles

Of evergreen weave
      To a teacup steeping one
            Egg. The male—who's mere

Ounces of purest
      Bullion except for those
            Dark-barred wings, that black

Yarmulke—chatters
      and chirrups and chitters as
            He fetches seeds to

Tempt his mate to eat,
      As she cozies one Alice-
            Blue egg, translucent

As the finest china,
        Flow blue from the Far East.
                As he sings and sings

And sings to her, I'm
        Reminded of all the hot
                And sour soup you served

That August when I
        Was great with child, our daughter;
                How to me, to her,

You sang and you sang,
        Sunday shirt bright beneath your
                Black suit, as you crooned

To me, as you crooned
        To our daughter, *These are*
                My girls, my girls, mine.

Blind Contour Drawing

      breast baby blanket unblinking
you on one side our daughter
      on the other an attentiveness
of hummingbird to trumpet
      vine her greedy honeysuckle
suckling your greedy flickering
      eyes as you drew us drew us
to you without ever looking away
      from me one continuous line
breast baby breast blanket blessing

Ulysses: *Uxoria*

Yes

After he told her
How he'd built their house around
That tree, after he

Described the dovetailed
Carpentry, bole cut off right
At the root, leaving

One leafy branch for
Bedpost, after he reminded
Her he'd planed the wood

Yes

Till it curved smooth as
Her hips, after he told her
How he'd laid in

Gold, silver, and strips
Of ivory pale as her
Skin, woven supple

Leather over its
Frame, ox hide gleaming red as
First blood—that deerhound

I said

Pinning a weak-kneed
Fawn, and what one might call
First-blooded—given her

The *sema,* sign, their own
Life story, he asked, "Is my
Bed still there, or

Has another uprooted
That olive tree?" Since she had
By now living proof,

    Yes I will

She knew him again
And again, as the olive
Tree that's their rooted

Bed flowers fullest
In this, its second decade,
As they delight in

Each other, as their
Sturdy bed blossoms in its
Continued cycle.

    Yes

In Ictu Oculi

My irises are blue,

Last November when winter came balmy,
      Unexpected, sabers thrust up through
           A scrim of gold gingko leaves, in early

milky with cataracts, still

December the last iris unfurled
      Its frills, sinuous scallops bisected
           Central from ciliary—blue ink pearled

I should have seen

From your fountain pen, blue lines crisscrossing
      Your atlas, blue veins traversing your wrist.
           An unseasonal gift that Christmas morning

the cyanotic nails, looked

Blossom on the white wicker tray—the vase
      That held the last iris was delicate,
           A milky blue. "There'll be more," you say, "next

more closely at your hands,

Spring. We'll have iris for years and years." Blades
      Of green slice through the earth this autumn,
           Your ashes in winter's bedded gardens.

not what they held.

Housewifery: An Annotation

To wash corsets: Take out the steel; use hot water;
one teaspoon of borax to every pail of water;
place the corsets on the washboard,
scrub well with a clean brush, using very little soap;
do not boil the corsets, but if very yellow bleach in the sun;
rinse well; rub in a little starch; iron when quite damp.
—Victorian Pamphlet

Artifact A: Corsets

Untightening the laces and unhooking the busk; I am on
(wash)board with this whole idea of containment. Now there's
no one tightening the laces or hooking the busk, or admiring
the torso so torqued, so misshapen, which I used to read as
miss-happen. And that's what happened—you miss-happened,
and honey I miss you.

Artifact B: Borax

20 Mule Team—that's what it took for me not to cast myself
in the fire with you, the stubbornness of 20 mules for me not
to go West with you; but part of me did, that day; most of me
burned that afternoon, as well; and the cupric-green flames
that borax produces when it's tossed into fire (the Emerald
City Green of the Wonderful Wizard) are the fires that stoke
me now, something naturally unnatural. When combined
with water, borax also bleaches, releasing hydrogen peroxide
bubbles into the boiling brew of the laundry kettle, quite the
opposite of bluing, and I am blue, *navy blue powder blue Alice*
blue wanting-to-rise-but-kept-down, hell, held-down blue without
you. All these shades are what Degas called "dead color."

Artifact C: Water

Takes on the shape of something else, of whatever it's put into;
the mattress has taken on your shape; I have taken on the shape
of a secret grief, that surprising containment, like pregnancy;
only instead of something growing, something's shrinking it's
my soul my smile my sense of self. *Eat me,* says the mushroom,
drink me, says the little flask, and like Alice, I never know how
grief will shape me next.

Artifact D: Place

A location, a gesture, the home you were and are to me. *Look
for me under your boot soles,* wrote Walt Whitman at the end
of *Leaves of Grass.* I look there. Not at home. I look above me
and see the curl of your curls in a cloud. *Cumulus,* you'd correct
me. Not there, either. In the plume of my breath after a cold
walk? No. I inscribe your name in the steam of the mirror. The
"H" looks just like the frame of a house going up. *No place like
home,* incants Dorothy. Without you, *home is no place.*

Artifact E: Washboard

Ribs. Ribbons. Ribaldry. Bone of my bone, and your bones
are now ash. I long for something-the scythe of a rib, the dice
of your knuckles. I would be your reliquary if you'd let me.
Corrugation of the tin roof of the old farmhouse, where we
made love by the fireplace. Rain falling heavy and my hair
falling over your face. *The only bridal veil you ever wore,* you
teased. I consign that memory to flame.

Artifact F: Well.

Wishing. Deep water. Cold water. Fare thee. Charon fares thee.
A four-letter word. Dark river. Cold river. Baptism. I am totally
immersed by this longing to plunge straight down into Styx.
They say from the bottom of a well you can see diurnal stars.
I look for the constellation of grief. I'd call it *Jailbait*, I'd call it
Honey, I'm home.

Artifact G: A Clean Brush

Wouldn't smell like your hair, when you had hair. (I have
your ponytail, a curly queue. It smells like sugar cookies and
cigarettes). Lately you'd kept your curls so short. Your hair
felt so moleskin sleek against my skin. I couldn't wash your
pillowcase for weeks, till the watermarks of my tears salted out
your scent. Vanilla wafting from an oven once made me weak
in the knees. Now I can't walk into Kirchhoff's Bakery without
having to spin on one heel and leave.

Artifact H: Do Not Boil

How can I not? I am bubbling over—a makeshift mutiny. I am
a cauldron, a caldera, a Calder sculpture in the wind. I am a
crucible and in a crucible. Throw in a little bluing, pull me out
with a pole, and send me straight through the wringer washer.
I'll emerge flat white, good as new. I'll be a doily, a dolly, a
pinafore hung in a closet with pantaloons and pomanders. I'll
smell very faintly of lavender, from *lavende,* meaning to wash.

Artifact I: Yellow

Ivory keys on the old piano. Your favorite shirt. The wild
canaries we saw at the park. You sang and sang and sang.
Miner's canary, you have gone before me. Your heart in its cage
of ribs. My finger in its wedding ring. Locket. You on one side
and me on the other. Gravestone.

Artifact J: Rub In

Or rub out. Erase. Rubbings over stone. Charcoal smudges.
Smudges on my fingers as I release you to the rose garden.
Fingerprint ink. Eyelash between finger and thumb. *Make a
wish,* you'd say. *I already had mine.*

Artifact K: Quite Damp

Damp? Tamp it down, put it in your pipe and smoke it. Suck
it up. Not to cry has been impressed on me from childhood.
Iron backbone, stiff upper lip. Now I've tears enough to turn
the Sahara oasis; I'm hard pressed to compress my distress.
I'm weighted between pages of the books you haven't finished
reading. We found four-leaf clovers and faded roses in the
brittle family Bible, discarded in a box outside the Goodwill,
the day we found our piano. *Someone lived,* you said, *and
someone else forgot.* I'll remember. Box of books, Bible, piano
with its missing black keys, missing pedal. Damper pedal:
Another word for it is sustained.

ONE WORD: *UNANSWERED*

derives from the words *against affirmation* those are its
        roots—a negative—and I think about all the emails you
never answered and all the phone calls you never answered
        and the letters that still come for you they fall through

the mail slot and there your name is at my feet someone calls
        and I don't answer and I think of how sometimes the cat
would listen as I played the answering machine over and over
        just to hear your voice *honey don't be mad but I stopped at*

the greenhouse again I still hear it sometimes in my head
        and that cat still runs downstairs whenever he hears
footsteps on the porch thinking it might be you and sometimes
        just for a moment I think it might be you too for years

now I've looked at the stars or a full moon and wondered when
        I'll get back to my old self or whatever you'd call
a self other times I notice that except for the cat and the ficus
        tree there are weeks I don't touch anything living at all

Months Later,
I Stand Here Ironing

my favorite white
        blouse with its embroidery
                of swallows swooping

among lilies; once
        you said God and some genius
                must surely have come

up with clothing
        for just this reason, *to leave
                a little something*

*on until I can
        take it off*... Ellipses of
                freckles dotted your

back, that blouse in the
        light dotted my clavicles...
                There are some secrets

I've never told, there are
        things that should stay (like that blouse)
                safe between a wife

and her husband, and
        yet... and yet today I found
                crushed in a closet

these swallows, these white
        lilies, fine cambric crumpled
                into ten thousand

wrinkles, where against
     your black cashmere coat it was
          pressed, as once it had

pressed against my breasts,
     as often in sleep they had
          pressed against your back.

TRIAGE

"Nothing is ever lost."
—Robert Penn Warren, *All the King's Men*

A cut into your eyebrow from a fall
Onto my bedpost, seven stitches so small
They were set in with a loupe. Cat's-claw nicks
On your left fourth finger—a cicatrix
Hidden under your class ring—trying to
Trap that tabby. Stigmata on your palms—you
On top of me in a flash in gravel,
Some muscle car backfired, and then you travel
Back to Khe Sanh. (I landed on green glass,
Heineken. The shards like floaters rise).
That caterpillar-shaped scar on your ass
From shrapnel. The scratches by your eyes
The mortician couldn't cover when you drowned.
Wounds I never sutured, closure I never found.

TO CLING TO

No Place like Home: 1965

Her bicycle and her broom, her fingers bony
As catfish barbels, skin the shade of scales
Scattered from the luna's wing—oh, the witch entire

Is what I craved—her pointed hat, her widow's
Weeds trailing behind her like a burning
Bride's veil, and her voice—pure power—

And your little dog, too. I mimicked
That rasping for days, and I was never
Afraid.... Never. What scared me were the trees,

Apple-laden branches that groped and grabbed,
False faces, wrinkling grey bark.... Trees like him,
Mr. Monday, who lived across the street,

Who clutched at my hair and my red car coat
When I wouldn't go back to the porch slanting
Before his pointy house. *Da duh, da duh*

Da duh—each lurching pair of steps was perfect
Iamb, a meter I'll scan again, again.
No one heard me shriek; my voice was too faint

To carry. Later, I didn't have words
To say what I cannot say. As I watched
The Wizard of Oz the weekend after,

Hexing, I called down my worst on him,
Curses like *poppies, poppies* that sent
Dorothy and the Cowardly Lion

To sleep, to sleep. *No one will wake him up;*
Mr. Monday lives alone, not even
A dog... Before the mirror, as I murmured,

I gazed at my unfamiliar face:
These things must be done delicately.
If they have ears to hear, then let them hear.

In the Laundry Room

Outside Hickman, Kentucky,
I am left with our maid
Annie (my grandma was

Out shopping) and I sit
And watch her iron in
This too-hot laundry room.

It is dark, and the room's
Hung full of shirts
With no arms in them,

Dresses, empty aprons.
Annie has been ironing
For what seems like forever

And while I wait I color
In my National Velvet
Coloring book, and I stay

Within the lines:
The girl with the hair
Of a boy, the horse

With the name of a pie.
They jump over sticks and
Over stones. I watch Annie

And her friend Cowboy
Who's working out in
Grandma's flowers—where

Dry petals fall, all colors,
Like my crayons. Annie
Has her Pepsi bottle

For sprinkling, and it's
Stoppered like a zinnia,
Or the watering can

Cowboy carries. In my box
Of 48 the colors line up
In rows like the roses

Cowboy tends. These
Crayon names are
Sometimes sticks, and

Sometimes stones. *Flesh*
Reads one, which isn't
The right color of me,

Or Cowboy; Annie, neither.
She's the color of Pepsi that
Once filled up that bottle,

He's more the shade of plums
That dry up in a dish
In Grandma's kitchen,

And I'm more the color
Of that dish. None of us
Is this funny shade

Of canned salmon
Annie presses into
Patties. Back when

I was little, we played
Patty-cake. The pink of her
Palms is pinker than mine,

Pinker than roses Cowboy's
Cutting. She's not flesh—that's
Just a label on a crayon, and

I'm not coloring Velvet. I'd
Rather watch Annie, who's
Ironing my best dress,

Which is velvet and black,
Which is not the color
The sky is turning, even

Though it is getting darker
And darker, and I've waited
Now so long. The iron steams

Hot cotton, and my crayons
Smell like birthday candles,
Lining up in two sections

Like at the movies, lower
And balcony levels (where
I never sit with Annie).

Annie is Grandma's girl,
And I am, too. And Cowboy
Is old, 48, like the crayons

In my box, and he's not
A boy, and also Velvet's
Not a boy. And I'm a girl

And colored, but not like
Cowboy or Annie. And
Still Velvet is not colored.

I'm afraid of going beyond
The thick outlines.
Finally, ironing's done,

All the wrinkles have been
Smoothed over, and now
It's time for Grandma.

Annie takes me downtown,
And I sneak up to her water
Fountain, expecting grape

Soda, or pink lemonade,
Or at the least some
Pepsi, but it's just plain

Water, not colored
At all, and on the way
Home, I'm mad and

I'm trying not to cry;
All the way home as
I look out the window

Everything—sky,
Houses, horses,
Roses—all the world's

Going grey, grey
As the ash from
Grandma's ivory

Cigarette holder as
She sits where she should
In the back beside me.

SHAME AT THE FIVE AND DIME

(for Persephone)

Hole burning in your pocket, like a small
Full moon, it's a sweat-slick
Quicksilver sliver of silver, and you

Have to spend it quick
Before you're caught and catch
Hell and brimstone... The notches

In the side of it notch up your sins.
Here are notions if you get a notion
For sewing, here are floss and flossy

Spools of scarlet, cinnabar, silver;
Here are the smallest safeties:
Pins clinging possum

To their mother's underbelly
(Kittens in a row, *kittens*
In a sack, she's said so);

Here's a sewing kit cunning
Enough to fit into your palm
Like this dime you stole

From your own mother's
Coin purse, round yellow
Plastic, no bigger than her

Rain bonnet—*Baptists*
Believe in Total Immersion
In gold gilt letters—

Gift from the Ladies' Auxiliary;
Here are hooks that don't catch
You lifting that silver,

Judas girl, Punch and
Judas, and also eyes
That won't witness;

Here are zippers
With their snaggle teeth
Keeping their secrets safe;

Here's a pincushion of ruddy
Love apples and strawberry,
Improbable vine, fine grit

For sharpening
Needles, for needling,
Doesn't fall far from the tree;

Here are needles from pin-eye
To tapestry to gaping
Carpet tacker (little Cyclops);

Here are ribbons to tie you
And tape measure with its
Black piano keys to play

Was lost but now am found;
Here is rickrack or hem tape
To stop threading topsoil

Into the silk of your hem
Coming undone, uneven
Shoreline; here's elastic thread

To slip-stitch your slip strap before
It's snowing down south when hell
Freezes over from one thin

Dime, the one that's branded
Your palm, Mercury dime, stolen
Silver, only one piece and not 30.

You spend it on embroidery
Transfer of daffodils to iron
On a handkerchief.

THE SIXTIES: AGE 10,
WHAT I WANTED WAS

my name to be poppy and not pamela;
                         wanted a mouth that wet, and a paper mini
dress and an Indian gauze skirt crinkly
                         as those petals; wanted a flop-brim hat and
go-go boots of white leather, I wanted
                         eyeliner and a black velvet choker,
a mary quant flower; a wiglet and lace
                         stockings; wanted baby doll-pajamas;
wanted to be thin as a sleeve, straight as
                         a twig; wanted tabs for all my clothes; nights
I wanted to be tucked inside a flap,
                         filed in a folder, flat as a flitter;
wanted straight hair so I ironed it,
                         wanted a flat chest; breasts sprouted anyway.

Eminent Domain

Somewhere under that bass boat is where her
Garden grew, beds thick with thyme, cat-tongues

Of catmint, and pansies there for nothing
But deep pleasure from their velvet faces.

Gran says to me, *You value that tap water.*
Dawns, she'd plod to the pump, then haul water

Downhill, past the cemetery where her
Confederate dead lay buried, where her

Father and his father and his father's
Father were baptized in the bend of Lost Creek,

Going in dry sinners, some of them coming
Up wet ones. They held lanterns, had moon and

Moonshine to light their paths. Gran says, *Now that
Indoor plumbing certainly surprised.* No more

Crescent-moon houses, no more rattlers
Coiled deep in kudzu, no more chiggers at her

Ankles along with her woolens. Over
That first ridge of pin oak and sycamore,

(Thirty feet underwater now), a sailboat scuds.
Its bright silks billow. Gran says, *Don't*

Hold your breath waiting on the government.
She's glad for the taps that turn cold to hot,

For the double sink, for the zinc stove, for
Electric cords knotted as ginseng roots.

Near nightfall, Gran pulls the lamp cord, says,
Let there be light. She says grace over fish, yet

What of floodlights that fill the dammed-up
Valley, what of drowned graves, lost creeks; what

Of churches (all of them Baptist now,
Converted by total immersion), what of

Tobacco barns and toolsheds
Sunk at the bottom of the man-made lake—

Gone with foundries, with memories
Of axe handle and plow tongue, wood plane and

Tobacco spike, soldier and Grandfather,
Garden and rosebush by the front gate—

And the front gate. I want to ask Gran, "What's
The right phrase for forgive and not forget?"

Is it *Eminent Domain? Rosemary*
For Remembrance? Rue's massed there in dirt

By her doorway, as out of place as that bleached-
Bone diurnal moon, clenched in the early

Afternoon haze hanging over the shore
Of Lake Barkley, knuckling under to the sun.

(for the families displaced by eminent domain, 1780-1969)

BREASTS

Figure A.   Woman, nude from the waist up, standing in front
                of mirror. Arms raised above head; breasts
                inspected for dimpling, thickening.

Tin tub, hot water hauled
        Steaming from the stove, steaming
                The mirror. Lye soap.

Flare of hips, bare back,
        Her hair slipping its awkward
                Snood, rippling past her

Shoulders. Left arm crooked
        Over head, that beautiful
                Tilt, that supplication.

Sponging off the sweat
        From packing pecans all day,
                Culling the kernels

At Roper Candies,
        Sponging under arms—downy
                Hair iridescent

With suds, sponging
        Under breasts. Looking down.
                19. Nipple. Nipple.

Figure B.   Woman face up, flat in bed, small pillow under left
                shoulder. Position prevents sagging, results in
                satisfactory inspection.

Reading in bed, learning
>The body the way the blind
>>Learn Braille, fingers against

Skin, scanning. Circling,
>Circling from the shoulder inward,
>>Inward. Fingers slick

With Jergens gliding
>Over the breast—water skate
>>Skimming the thin skin

Of the pond—spiraling
>Inward like a nautilus,
>>Stippled, thicker here.

39. Hackle. Hackle.

Figure C.   Recent radical mastectomy showing markings for
radiation. Incisions placed so that they will not show
when wearing evening dress or bathing suit.

Suturing, suturing,
>Interrupted silk. The scar
>>Crosshatched, diagonal

From shoulder to her
>Xiphisternum. Zipper, zipper.
>>Something's wrong with this

White leather, this
>Epidermis sliced and scraped
>>And stitched—no nipple,

No tissue, no muscle,
      No lilt—skin stretched like canvas
            Over washboard ribs.

She can see straight down to
      Her pubis. It hurts to zip
            Her dress, brush her hair.

She used to be quite
      The seamstress, hands darting here and
            There. No pattern now.

49. Radical, radical.

Figure D.   Table showing statistical survey of definite
                tendency toward the development of breast cancer
                cancer among family members.

Spring's sprung, I'm ten, I
      Don't ever want to get tits—
            I've seen my grandmother

Changing clothes, changing.
      She didn't know I was watching
            Her, watching. I'd gone

Outside, climbed up in
      The pear tree, its dark branches
            Weighed down with a pearly

Spray of bloom. I'd shaken
      Its limbs, bruised its thick clouds
            Of blossom, littered

The ground with petals.
          Pollen fell all over me,
                    A layer of gold, gilding

Gilding. Something's changed.
          I can smell the sweet rot of
                    Bloom, can hear the bees

Buzz as they suckle, see
          For the first time how each petal
                    Isn't pure white but

Curled at each edge, pale brown.
          Someday I'll need a bra, some
                    Day I'll sag like Gran.

Not me. Not now.

Figure E.   Pathologist inspecting each slide of fine needle
                 aspiration carefully for basal cell changes. His role
                 is vital in the preservation of the woman's breast.

My boyfriend at work:
          White walls, white rats, white lab coat,
                    White hands adjusting

The lens. He works as
          A pathologist, sifting
                    Through slides for changes

In cells, staining them
          Violet, murmuring words like
                    Metastasis, like

Carcinoma. Low
    In the throat, almost purring.
        This is what it looks

Like; this is a textbook
    Case of CA, he says. And,
        Sometimes when I can't

Find anything, I
    Stay here half the night. I like
        To find it, like to

Find it. He's been my boyfriend
    For weeks now, *lover, lover,*
        He keeps telling me

You've got terrific lungs.

Figure F.   Mammogram showing stellate lesions, suspicious
            for breast cancer. Note the clusters, in pairs.

Daughter, we're rocking
    And at my breast you tunnel,
        Tugging, tweaking, your

Little mewlings a pleasure
    As unexpected as this ringing.
        Whoever's calling

At 2 a.m.? I'm
    Thinking of carnage. It's my
        Baby sister. *I have*

Stage IV, stage IV, and
      Can you come right out? Between
           Our phones, there's the roar

Like the ocean's, as
      If we were holding shells up
         To our ears, a song

Not unlike the blood's.
      She's only 40. *Tattoos.*
         Radiation markings.

Ablation. Neither
      Of us will say *cancer,*
         Neither of us

Mentions our mother.
      Daughter, I hold you tighter
         To my breast.

I Stand Here Ironing:
A Fairy Tale

The iron shrieks its one note—E—a high-
      Pitched sound: the difference between singing
And singeing. The setting's on Permanent

Press, not Silk, not Shot of Steam—we'd
      Experimented with it once: clouds sent
Straight to the scalp might scald. *Nobody loves*

Crimps, crinkles, wrinkles, and waves like ours, you say.
      (1972 and nobody
Knows about our hair). You want yours satin-slick,

These tresses we finally grew after years
      Of haircuts (an inch off for every sin)
That left you pixie and me almost bald.

I had less hair than a nun. Rosemary, how
      It's my role to remember, to smooth things
Over…. You face the ladder of the chair

Back, kneel over the rails—like the crones
      In church—they call it *genuflect.* My arm
Moves back and forth, some strange blessing the priest

Waves over the Host, which is the Body
      Of Christ. Your body's straight, your head's turned in
Profile. Cameo, new coin, you'll turn heads soon.

On my arms hide arrowheads, triangulating
      Points, deltas that mark the start of
My iron age. Each one's prehistory, hard signs

That mark the past: I charred Father's shirt
　　　　Collar, singed pillowslips, scorched percale, was
Paid in kind by Mother. I never burned

You, Sister. When I press your yard-long hair
　　　　It slips out straight, fine, yellow as butter.
Each strand's spun true as Rumpelstiltskin's thread.

You'll marry the prince, we're sure. I've wound
　　　　My hair in plaits; I keep it tightly bound.
I want to be Rapunzel, fairest one

Of all… but I only unravel forward for you.
　　　　For you, I'll sing songs, if it takes me years,
I'll spell the words, undone: *Singed. Scalded. Scalped.*

Sister, you're not here to hear my voice, it's
　　　　Shrieking like the steam iron, the kettle gone
Past boiling point. Sister, I can't keep you,

Though I want to press you like a flower
　　　　In our *Blue Book of Fairy Tales,* discover
You improbably blooming between

The pages, Gretel going home, safe at
　　　　Last within the woods. Sister, we always
Knew the story would close this way: One of us

Gone, the other one left to end it.
　　　　You told me that last day (all your hair gone,
Burned away in radiation tattoos),

You told me I had to write it down. *Say*
　　　　My name, sister, say my name. Tell them no,
Not happily ever after; you set

The record straight, tell everyone; write No,
*   Write it enough, write till enough's enough.*
Sister, we broke the spell. Our daughters are

Lovely, loved. We changed the ending, told them
        Tales of mothers without years of secrets.
Sister, I think it's enough to say *we lived.*

Poor-Mouthed Poem Composed During a Spring Storm

Goose feather pillows
    And duvet be damned. And that
Quilt of my great-aunt's

Dresses, each flour-sack
    Cotton or calico worn
Thread by thread to bare

Kapok over my
    Shoulders (oil-slicked to rainbow,
For what exactly?

—No one touches me,
    Not even when they touch me)—
Burn it, too. And burn

Me, though cremation
    Won't warm me; even calcite
Constellations of

My bones won't be
    White enough, bright enough. And
Exactly how far

Away is the light
    Of the star where you promised
You'd wait? Sheet lightning

Is false light. I quake
    In its silence, its sizzle,
The sheets wind round me.

Unchained Melody:
The Studio Version

"I hunger." —Bobby Hatfield

Cashmere sweater slung over the arm of a sofa;
      Grey beard of dust
      Festooning a single sock
(Yes, each of the argyles is a clock without hands);

Pale parallelogram over the winged-open *Dictionary*
      Of Difficult Words, pages
      Spanning *votive* to *vulva,* their
Origins *flame* to *sheath*—literally, *shroud.*

Soot, pollen, paint, pastels—all but dust;
      Books, chalk, inkpots,
      Canvas, crayons—all but dust;
Ashes to ashes and the skin just dust

Cover for the moons and boats, carpals that slipshod
      Sail through the wrist's canals,
      Sinew and the strong
Teeth and the tongue that spoke these words:

When everything is over, I want to be over
      Everything. For the bones
      That blackened
Quickly, for the green fires that were

Your eyes, for the gold spokes within them, for praise
      Of everything that made you curio
      Cabinet, natural wonder,
I save everything: papers, nubbins of pencils,

Myself. I wrap this kimono around my body
> As tightly as a dust jacket
> Enfolds a book—
Not any book, but *The Floating World,* that last gift

You gave me. I inhabit a world afloat—no, not
> The body erotic but the body
> That's drifting from your burnt-
Away body; body of flotsam, jetsam, body of rain;

Body alive like Danaë in a personal cloud
> Of gold coins, tens
> Of thousands of them,
Nonpareils, in air the size of a sugar cube,

Speck after speck speckling the surfaces
> With constellations,
> Galaxies that might be
You. I trace your name on the desktop.

SOMETHING TO DECLARE

Documentary: The thick flat brushes,
The glass of water gone grey with color,
The rough white paper, then your deft salvage
Of the smudges I'd made; how you told me
About accident, about chance and balance;
How you bit your lip as you worked; how quickly
We went to bed. *Like air,* you said. *You can
Never get enough.* Later, you painted
Me in oils, the fluorescent lights leaching
The color from my skin, my mouth a gash
Of Persian red—and, after you're gone, I couldn't
Bear to sell it. In my garage now, it's stored
Beside that pair of Japanese herons:
Red-capped, stilted, the ones that mate for life.

TO CLEAVE

A CAPPELLA

(*I was there*, insists the self).

Surprising and sufficient
       In the silence, just enough
           Luster for them

To be seen, street light
       Falling in bars across the bed,
           In wavering

Curving clefs across their
       Bodies, right now they are this
           Lovely: lovers,

Light—lying face to
       Face, working the long seam
           Between them, blurring,

Becoming faceless,
       Facelessly beautiful,
           A music of lilting

Ribs, torsos all thrust
       And ache. (*I really was there*,
           Insists the self.

Insist, insist).

78 RPM

Dusk and three minutes
Of fading light,

Pale as moonflowers,
Muted trumpets now,

Drawn up tight as those
Parasols propped in

The corner of your aunt's
Screened-in side porch, which

She calls *the veranda,* where
White wicker bites

Through your white cotton
Shift, as she lifts a disk

Of black scratchy "wax,"
Places it on the Victrola,

Says, *I'll be back in
A shake, you two,* and

Disappears inside.
As the heavy arm angles

From left to right, as
The stylus traces

Its sapphire finger
Down the record's groove,

As he skates a single
Finger along the sun-

Bleached down of your
Arm, and as you

Start to shake,
Heart rising and

Falling like Billie's
Song, cool water poured

To the top, brimming,
Then spilling silver

Notes, and his lips
On yours for—

The stylus bumps
Its paste-paper

Center; you hear
The screen door's

Thump against its
Frame, hear Aunt's

High heels tick
Across the porch.

Here's something
For this heat,

She says, handing you
Each iced tea: beaded

Glass, mint and a
Paper umbrella

Blooming, a drink he
Grasps quickly and gulps.

You'll have to keep your
Knees pressed tight together.

As the light dims.
As the record changes.

Unslaked

(after Song of Solomon 5:5)

I wanted to write something complicated,
    something curious, something cultivated
        as the manicured gardens of Versailles,
            something espaliered against the page

like the alphabet of those roses torqued
    against the palace walls; I wanted you
        to know I'm so sophisticated
            I've translated the Song of Solomon

on just my nerve and a dictionary...
    But when I'm thinking of you I'm not so
        complicated, not so cultivated, not
            so sophisticated; I've never been

to Versailles (unless you count the one
    in Kentucky); none of my roses is trellised,
        either—they meander over fences,
            I've never been able to prune them back;

and as for translation I've been stuck
    on chapter and verse (5:5), and I've tossed
        the dictionary down and nearly crushed the cat.
            And now I can't think of anything—French

Revolution or walled-off gardens or
    the English word for the Hebrew word
        for *awakening*—I've nothing to say
            that's more complicated than the weather,

and besides it hasn't rained here; the roses
    are drooping, as parched for water as I
        am parched for words. And so I put down my
            pen and paper, pick up the garden hose.

And after I've watered the roses, muddied
    their mulch so they're wetter, after I've
        washed my hands of both garden and poem
            and all those impressive words that won't

impress you (won't impress on you just why
    I want to impress you); as the water
        beads over my wrists and runs dripping down
            my fingers, I realize that I'm not more

complicated than this, what falls and flows
    over my hands, I want to move as
        effortlessly toward you as the water
            moves from shore to shore, I want

to open to you like a book opens, show you
    the calligraphy of my hair as it slips out
        of its French braid and waves against my back....
            I've forgotten to turn off the water, it's dripping

everything's drenched and spilling over;
    I finally have it—garden, roses, and locks,
        the word I need to unlock Solomon, trace
            it from right to left in the dirt: *Aroused.*

CAMEO: EPITHALAMION

Cheekbone, chin, chignon;
      Scrollwork, a profile carved in
           Worn carnelian,

Russet and ivory;
      Only a blur remains, there
           Where her ringlets were;

Here, a tiny crack feathers
      To the speck of stone
           Hidden in the hollow

Of her throat, the ribbon
      Strung with its diamond.
           Great-Aunt Beatrice's

Brooch, ornament she wore
      In her own wedding, now
           Pinned to my bodice

That feels like peach skin.
      Velvet, velvet, the nap one way,
           Cannot be touched

Against the grain.
      Mannequin, mannequin,
           Here I stand in

Off-white, with statice
      Snarled in my hair, hot
           Under the umbrella lights

Of the photographer,
    On the day before my marriage.
        I can't breathe—how this

Velvet loops me tight,
    Wraps my torso, cocooning me,
        Like the caterpillars,

Swaddled in kapok, whose
    Tents swathe the vee of the wild
        Plum….. This dry champagne's

A shade so pale,
    The same tint as the sheaves
        That spill open, heavy

Vellum, falling
    Gracefully between Malachi
        And Matthew, between

Old and new. Sepia
    Script, penned in various
        Hands, catalogues those

Birthed, dipped, wed, and gone.
    There's a line where our names
        Will go—brownish,

Blotched with age, like Great-
    Aunt Beatrice's hands as they
        Pinned this on me,

The bride. *Blank page.*

First Anniversary: Reading Russian Literature

No money, so we sip from glass cups niched
In silver holders; I show you how my
Grandmother kept cubes of sugar between
Her teeth, *to make life sweeter;* I'm reading

Some dead poet (not *Zhivago*), tracing
Words—*samovar, nyet,* and the quicksilver
Cyrillic letters twining round the rust-
Dappled canister: Russian Caravan.

How our skin's slicked with sweat—too hot to
Sleep (or even stand); how all we can
Afford is this: back porch, spiked tea, spotting
These slugs. Each pair's a heat-slick valentine,

Drooping below the bleeding hearts you snitched
From a neighbor's garden—swollen pouts that
Blossom in shadow—and, like slugs, salt will
Melt them both. Sugar cube, teacup, mottled

Little leopards, milk-blue tin, pearls of heat,
Fringed branches, slow-swaying swing. You wish, like
A child at Christmas, for snow; *I loved you
Hopelessly* is all I remember of Pushkin.

Taking a Walk with You

"Walk forwards and backwards with me." —*Kenneth Koch*

Gazing into Wet
Creek's tapestry, through
The warp and weft of

Minnows weaving
In shafts of sunlight, echoed
In the shadows of

The sawgrass swaying,
In the small stream's undulance
Toward the river

Torqueing to the Ohio
That somehow will spill
Into the Atlantic,

All salt spray hissing
Against rocks: the sound of
Repeatable longing.

That's there. And here a
Cardinal calls *Pretty*
Pretty Pretty from

The pin oak, here a
Woodpecker strikes its match-
Head against old elm

Bark, here the creek widens and
Narrows. Dear, the stents in
Your heart wend the same;

The plate and screws in my knees
Tell me before the skies do
How there'll be rain, drops

Canting crazily,
Pocking the creek. The bodies
We have are also bodies

Of water, bodies of dust, bodies
That change like clouds, bodies
That will fill, and fail,

And fall. *That's later.* Now as we thread
Our way through cattails
In gauzy light, there's this

Pause, an inrush of breath, holding
It, holding your hand
Watching the water, the way

It flows, feeling my body moving
Toward yours, as the water reflects us
As we were then, in its

Mottled plane, *Mirror,*
Mirror, our younger
Faces gazing back

At us from their side
Of this day, as we work our
Way, through cattails, through

Muscadine, weaving through scything
Sawgrass, sumac, taking the path
Of least resistance.

Here Lies

Flat on my back in grass—child's bed,
Matelassé quilt —white lilies, clipped,
Wait in wet newsprint beside me

(Scent of them infusing the want
Ads, the black hems of obituaries);
Your old hat covers my face.

This would be the best day for it:
Sunlight, sieved through straw,
Then spun to gold through windows

In the weave, prisms my eyelashes;
Pruning's done, and in grass I'm
Languid, lying down alone as I

Have been over and over; once
Again I wish over me the earth
Would gently fold her fingers,

Would cover me in the basket
Of her hand, as I've held a firefly
At last light, a cold peridot lantern.

Halo of straw crowning my head,
Gold band cinching my finger,
Ring of your ashes round the garden.

Willingly, I'd be Persephone, go
Into the nether land, grass bent
For a time to silhouette where

I was or wasn't. Wrapped in words,
These lilies, blossoms I scythed
For you, would wait, abandoned.

Materials and Not Enough Time: An Alphabet

Alençon lace (I see you through a veil)
Broadcloth (the prairie sprawls and undulates)
Burlap (kittens in a sack you rescue them)
Calico (aprons and flour sack frocks cut up for your quilt)
Cambric (handkerchief of the Lord, I embroider an H)
Canvas (an artist's model shivers in the corner, the artist
    is you the model is me)
Chino (you called them your lawyer pants, wore them when
    you were permanently pressed for funds)
Cotton (your skin my skin same boll)
Corduroy (kings' cloth, Thomas Hart Benton's furrowed fields,
    fretted like your old Gibson) Crepe (my 1920s *de chine*
    dress cut on the bias, flowers over my hip bones, petals
    and branches over my ribs),
Denim (your thigh sliding through the wicket of mine
    in the doorway where we first kissed),
Felt (wetting wool, rubbing wool, a congress of wet sheep
    in an Irish pub we visit),
Flannel (your shirt still warm from your skin, I steal it for
    a quick trip to the kitchen)
Fleece (I have been shorn of you)
Gabardine (your three-piece suit with its vest, its watch chain
    and fob, the suit I couldn't bury you in)
Gauze (Breathing through it, seeing through it after you're gone)
Gingham (cheery kitchen curtains with cross-stitched
    roosters, I am scrambling the first eggs I'll make for you)
Kapok (we are cocooned together, a private tent in the cherry trees)
Lamé (drag queen who made you laugh your lustiest
    at "You're Not Woman Enough to Take My Man,"
    the swaggering hips of the singer, the waterfall of gold
    over them)

Linen (the tan and black suit I wore on our first Easter,
  the one that fits again because I can't eat/don't cook
  without you)
Madras (a plaid we didn't like, a city we wanted to visit)
Muslin (that impossibly thin antique blouse, leg o'mutton
  sleeves and lace collar on which you pinned for me
  a cameo)
Nylon (your thumbnail sends a millipede skittering down my
  stocking)
Organza (the sheer fabric, the topnotes of gardenia
  in a perfume you picked out)
Piqué (the screen door, slamming behind us as we head
  to the lake, fishnets)
Rayon (the 1940s dress I wore when we'd swing dance,
  you'd lift me and I'd fly)
Satin (slick sheets you'd throw off the bed)
Serge (the ocean's undertow, all these layers stitched together)
Silk (one of the few fabrics that will shatter, as mirrors do,
  as I have)
Twill (classic fabric, archaic contraction, twill never be better)
Velvet (the feel of your skin, there)
Voile (close to veil, my hair over my face, my dress over a chair)
Wool (it made you itch, so I would scratch your back)
Worsted (these days the way they're woven, warp
  and weft and what's looming)

WIDDERSHINS

You come to me in a dream that's a wash of grey over pen and ink lines (Koh-I-Noor ones you loved to draw); you're wearing your pearl-grey suit because grey suits you; your hair curls like smoke, the way it did when you smoked, you ask, *Pamela, do you see me? I haven't been this thin in years!* You're flat black construction paper; silhouetted against the garden, a man twirling a cane in a Kara Walker landscape; you tell me you're perspective, you're negative space, you're an old negative in an envelope of deckle-edged photos; the dark triangles that will hold them in an album are scattered before you like so many Escher birds; they will scatter and wing to the four corners of what has become my earth, your berth. You're insubstantial as ash at the end of a cigarette, still suggesting a shape before it falls or before it's tamped out in a tray; you're the flimsy rectangular box that holds your ashes, the starbursts of your bones; you're the alphabet of ash I scatter and then tamp into the garden; you have become no more and no less than you wanted—*H, E, P*—you have become a man of letters that you'll never write; you have been swallowed by the shade of the gingko and its fans, you have become caught in the dreadlocks of the willow, in the needles of the pine and the thread of the garden spider as she begins to spin her orb; you leave behind only a memory of your words—your postscripts, your calligraphy—as I spill more and more of ashes around the mulch-black bed of iris, the faint furrows of day lilies, in haloes around the trellis twined with roses; these are the lines I imagine that I've penned and inked as I walk widdershins in the garden, against the rotation of the seasons, countering the clocks; as I dress in your black sweatshirt, in your black ball cap; as I carry your shears, your scythe, your ashes, as I scatter even more of you, *north south, south north, right left, left right*, till I am left to write.

IT PAYS TO INCREASE YOUR WORD POWER: *DIMINUENDO*

clover
cover or lover
over

Bee respondent above *clover*, clover as ground *cover*, bee as *lover* who leaves the clover, the finality of *over*, not as in bee from clover but the causality of cleaving.

cleave
leave
eave
Eve

The infinitive is Janus—*to cling to* or *to sever*, to clasp as the girl drowning holds to the mast; to split along a natural fault line. This is how we cleaved—I no longer aligned myself against your back; at 3 a.m. you no longer turned to cup my breast. The whole seismography of home has cracked to house, and I am left useless as gingerbread trim rick-racking the eaves, of the period but peripheral; I am left with fundament, with pediment, with other architectural salvage; I pick up what I can and preserve it but whatever leaves, leaves. I am in this garden with statuary and salvia, but there is no tree of knowledge I can find, no apple beckoning among the leaves, although certainly there are any numbers of copperheads.

cloven
coven
oven

The devil has left his mark in the earth outside my window—
too big for a deer, and only one hoof print next to a boot sole
mired in mud. We could take a perfect cast of it, if we had
plaster of Paris, and if we were still a *we* and not just an *I*.
Sometimes I feel like an evil eye, I do I do. I could call out for
others like me; I could convene a coven with the dozen bees
caught in the trapdoors of the foxglove.

The sun bakes these tracks to a brick, and I dig it up and put it
in a pot. I wonder how long I'll have this mark of Old Nick on
my porch. I wonder what I have unearthed.

clove
love

I remember the sizzle and hiss of your clove cigarettes—
Kretek—and the taste of them on my tongue as your
tongue eased into my mouth. After you, kissing is for nieces
and weddings and is just a parenthetical move for dates. I
understand kisses now that they no longer act as anodyne, now
that my life is no longer studded with them.

~~lover~~
over
over
over

I look at *pomander* differently, too, an apple embossed with cloves, a scent I love. How we'd lie together at the lake, your curls against my breasts. The carapaces of cicadas, the segmented bodies of cryanoids embedded in limestone; lawn chairs blue-green as lichen, our Song of Songs translation over coffee and sugar cookies. Cleavage, how you loved it when my locket slipped. *I'd be happy in there forever,* you laughed. Your photo's embedded in its frame; it still slithers between my breasts, and that sterling heart won't stay shut. I snap the frame, lock up the locket, and the reliquary opens again to show us both sequestered. What's left of my heart is a sprung gear. Like the artificial nightingale, music is just not quite right these days, although the tune still plays if I wind it up.

Victorian Ladies Once Read in the Dark by Tracing Raised Type on a Book's Pages

And I recall by rote every pore, every
                    pockmark, every iris fleck
of gold and green; drift of your lids as
                    you'd slip into sleep; moons of your
fingernails pared close—how it becomes
                    you, and I recreate your image
as surely as if out of carnelian I'd carved
                    a cameo, or pulled paper wet
from the developing tray, as you did
                    in your first studio with its attached
darkroom, the light gone silver in
                    your photographs—ephemera of gnats,
filigree of spider webs strung with dew.
                    I learned from you of Rossetti's
beloved, how she'd read books in the dark,
                    fingertips so sensitive she'd feel slopes
and ridges of type come alive under
                    her hand, as light flickered, died down,
winked out. And isn't it underhanded, too,
                    what death does, how it proves nothing
is safe—we're born, spilled into
                    light like a photograph, and then all
light leaches out, and we're ash and ink—
                    and our dark rooms become even
darker, doors shut and me shut out, shut
                    in—nights when I cut off everything: all
my friends and, once, my hair; waves fell
                    to the floor in *S*'s and *C*'s—you loved their

curves like cedillas. In French *tomber*

means *to fall,* and this fall, four years after
you fell, curved petals molt from

chrysanthemums white as your black curls
in the negative of our wedding portrait.

Like your curls, my waves, like water,
time slipped right through our fingers.

I think of women braiding the locks of
their beloved into brooches, dyeing

plumes of ostrich ebony, of letters
rising under whorls and eddies of

their fingertips. *Cedilla, tear, rivulet,*
river, sea. And now I waver, this side

of the Styx, now I try my best not to
look back, now that I'm not looking

forward to anything. My fingers fumble for
the repoussé locket that holds a braid

of your hair, our very first photograph together.
Under my fingers I trace crosshatchings

chased around its sterling heart. I don't look at
your photo; I never thought it looked

a thing like you, and now I feel it does.

Dendrochronology: A Definition

ring where my wedding ring was

ANYTHING IN THE THICKET

"We like a fire and we don't mind if it smokes."
—Gertrude Stein, *Lifting Belly*

What I touch flash-burns; what I leave turns
        Into ash.
Or *I'm sorry for myself,* or *I*
        Disagree
With myself, or *How I miss my last*
        Lover—cold,
Stoned, and partial to me. Now he
        Doesn't come
Anymore, now it's night, now here you
        And this fire
Arrive, best of all and worst of all. I
        Don't much like
A fire tonight, and the same goes for
        Death. I like
You smoking, here in bed, your black hair
        And darker
Thoughts of consumption and no light, to
        Which I don't
Agree. Smoking, your hands are strangers. And
        Again this
Fever, stoked, goes up. I learn some things
        Here, a lot
Of your words: *Welcome Heartbreak;* we welcome
        All the things
That do the breaking as our cigarettes
        Wither in
Their trays. Elegies? I understand them
        Better now.

My Name Once Meant

Aftermath:

Forget your name;   forget the time,
moon is full.   She calls out to you:
nothing but the   scent of beeswax.
Anne to blonde,   Saffron threads,
its gear. Farmers   in yellow almanacs
up, the ghost, the ring,   the name, give up
give up on him,   and give him up.

Bestirring:

Bee-stings, itchy   hives, mercury rises
thermometer. That   *Strawberry Moon* reddens
bite your beestung   lower lip till it bleeds.
of heat, July with its   sparkers like stars,
of *pollen pistil sepal*   brings you to; it
the ceiling fan.   Restless, decide to
into rumpled angels.   ***Confess, confess.***

Cornucopia:

September falls away   to fall; gingkoes
their gold kimonos.   Insinuating through
Her Bonnet. Cliché   *in the Harvest Sky.*
sleep under a hex   of quilts. Add
hiver, word for   winter, diminished
bitten arc, that   toe pick at the end
tips of his teeth,   like a comb's, as your

COMB OF SWEETNESS

try to forget he's
Old Crone. Know
Buff the the floors of
daffodil ruff, and
can fortell it—
the gifts in their
This space intent-

gone. Remember the
nothing, honey,
your old Queen
spring has sprung
Lenten Moon. Give
bright cocoons;
ionally left blank.

from the silver
the sky. Pile your
Moon, Swoon, June.
July with its litany
brings to you the
spread your wings;
Sin of omission.

dollar in the old
hair atop your head;
July with its haloes
of *lilies, lilies, lilies,*
hagiography of
work percale sheets
Sin of commission.

he planted for
every branch is
Shiver under your
to hive the murmur
shiver with its *S*
of your skates.
tongue riffed over

you shrug off
susurration. *Bee in*
ceiling fan's halo,
of *R* and learn
frozen, that coin's
Remember the sharp
their stings. **Stings.**

Da Capo Al Fine:

December offers   you solstice, if
remember that some   of the moves you
Inscribe figure-eights   into the scrim of
eternity; maybe it   figures — what all
drunk on the premise   of years and years;
maybe it's longing: how long you'll have
back up. **OBJECTS**   **ARE LARGER THAN**

Epiphany:

Restring the pearls   you snapped in a fit
flakes, white bees   bestirring a cloud.
Call yourself *Queen*   *Who Lives Through*
to Let, call yourself   perfected in the pond's
the moon's just   your own tarnished
your house when   the sky is clotted
sleet. Await your   own catasterism.

Full Circle:

Give up on that   moon; in dreams
name. You wouldn't   come, even if he
sweetheart, even if   he called you
almanac brings you   back around to
a little more. Know   the day, the month,
starve yourself into   a satin dress. Remember
Star, you break his   *heart.* Oh, break, heart,

not solace. Skate
have learned are
the pond. Maybe
he promised you,
maybe it's that long,
to wait here, honey,
THEY APPEAR

at night, pirouette;
compulsory.
it's for, or maybe it is
flushed with kisses,
maybe it's so long,
for your hive to fill
IN MIRROR.

of pique, think of
Say your name more
Winter, call yourself
mercury glass.
image, *Light Thief.*
with stars; make
Pleiades, One star

a swarm of snow
often, a rosary.
Vacant — Offices
Understand that
Pseudonym. Slip from
wishes that sting like
imploded.

and in your bed,
called you, even
burnished like wax.
Full Hunger. Drink
the year. Buff your
Miss Havisham,
break. **Honey's no**

no longer moan his
if he called you
That yellowing
a little less. Know
skin to bones, spindle,
who told Estella *Little*
longer a birthright.

Here Lies One: Remembering You Through Cavafy

And if you

After 25 years, return to sand, to silver glints
    Of gum wrappers and lead weights on broken
        Test line, return to the spot where he removed

Your swimsuit so deftly and posed you there
    And drew you to him after he drew you, your
        27-year-old body, in India ink with a wash of grey

At twilight, the magic hour when the sky's
    Violet, when the first stars pock it like rain on water
        And below them the lake lies, zinc, and waves are

Wrinkles looking for someone's brow—but not yours,
    For you'll be ink on ivory forever—and unchanged.
        What you didn't realize is that ivory cracks and after

Find her poor

He dies at this same spot where you were first filled
    Up with his child a quarter of a century ago you yield,
        You crack and craze; you unravel like fishing line or

Shot silk or kapok; you float into the air, into the water;
    Waves wash over you then, when grief finally beaches
        Itself like a hull in your heart's drift. The lake

Laps back and forth and fossils wash up in shoals,
    And a bass leaps, flares silver and green, and falls…
        And after you cry, you slip out of your swimsuit

And you look at your breasts that pleased one man
      And two children, at your belly that cocooned them,
            At the scar that he kissed when you first made love

Ithaka

After your C-section and you were shy, when he said
      It is coming home o it is—the only sure things now are
            Breast belly crescent scar—this is you, this is

Your body, and can this body so set in its ways
      Please another, will another wander to find you
            And feel at home? And you slip into the water

As though you were slipping back into your slip and
      You float and it is satin shock it is cold and clinging
            And your breasts bob and your hair's gilt

In the late afternoon sun and you cry just a little more
      And you climb on the rock where you once lay
            On top of him and you lie there till you're warm

Won't have fooled you

And you leave off your sundress, your sapphire slip,
      Your sandals (each dribbling sand like an hourglass),
            Your sunglasses, your St. Christopher, you gather

Them up in a towel, and naked you walk to the water.
      Your face wavers, and his words echo, and you do
            See that maybe there is still something to you,

Something of the figurehead—bare-breasted, ravaged
      By wind and wrinkling waves, a difference
            That perhaps he still sees, and you promise you'll

Learn to promise to love and honor and cherish
      Someone else, and you scatter the last of his ashes
            And scratch his name in the sand and watch.

Process Through Which My

Bone black pigments differ materially
in their intrinsic qualities. Each is
charring to blackness, in a closed
closed vessel, the material which
forms its base.

*A Treatise on Architecture and Building
Construction, Volume 3, Prepared for
Students of the International Correspondence
Schools, 1899*

prepared by charring
      bone or horn, whilst in the absence
          of air—deepest black

not used so widely
      as charcoal. Fragments, turnings
          of ivory, or

ore, or osseous
      orts of animals cuaght up
          in a crucible

encircled by coals
      combusted, and covered. Bones
          or calcium, when

BELOVED BECOMES A DIAMOND

Separate out NO MORE THAN 8 oz
(about 1 Cup) of the cremated prepared by
and tightly secure in a plastic bag or
other plastic container. DO NOT
send all the remains.

**We only need ounces to produce
all of the LifeGem diamonds on
your order.**
                    (LifeGem.com)

black lung baby rattling breath &
yr. baby teeth yr. thumbnail parings
iris and eyelash (thumb, forefinger)

narrow that reliquary
the turn of an eyetooth
the one I'd give to keep you—

oar in the water
Cerberus in the gondola
to hell that triangle of skulls

brimstone broomstraw you draw
from the broom to test the cake
yellow as a piano key

exposed to such heat, are
thus reduced to charcoal. This
16th-century

recipe calls for
a crucible surrounded
by charring coals, and

small bones, carpals, wax-
white or ivory, teeth and tusks,
wild boar, elephant—

covered closely, then
reduced in roux to charcoal.
When no more smoke

flames through the joint
of the cover, the crucible
should be left over

the flame for half an
hour or longer, or until
it has completely

cooled. There will then be
hard carbonaceous
matter, which, when

pounded and pestled
on porphyry to powder,
then sifted through seives,

forms the darkest of angels,
Rembrant's own shade for shadow.
From bone, other matter.

Intense Pressure Yields Hardening,

burning up baby too hot
briquette in the burner, incense
censering, confessional fingers knit together,

censoring I would call your name
(we both would come)
press a burning coal unto my lips

seal the bargain, come out right
those Shakers, dancing ecstasy,
angels on the head of a pin

wings spreading in out, fingers again
Cave art records the first yearnings
breathes in, breathes out, Lamaze, the maze

the cave's own allegory come out
come out ollie ollie oxen free
wherever you are

I'm not there, only half without you,
the hours fly like angels right by,
flown, & the dark seraph doesn't come

my name not written by yours
skull & crossbones (crossed my legs
& my fingers) a promise not kept

I meant it I thought that I would die
without you drown in Alice's own
tears. Any man's death diminishes me

but yours most of all. Handkerchief
tipped in black widow's weed
white flag of surrender, it matters

Hence a Diamond

CODA: OUT OF

my memory an entire bolt
        of fabric out of my memory
a boat with a leak or a sieve

or a sluice out of my memory
        a D-minor air whistled in
the dark past the combs-teeth

of tombstones out of my memory
        a pump with its needle prodding
a valve for the deflated tire

of my body out of my memory
        a spoked wheel turning out of my
memory a redaction *that tire's*

flat as a flitter out of my
        memory my daughter her hand
gripping the stub of a pencil

and *nubbin I think is a word*
        out of my memory a wave's
slow erasure out of my

memory she waves she pedals
        her bicycle out of my sight out
of my memory *no it was*

art class her white eraser over
        even whiter paper erased her
palimpsest my me mori

ACKNOWLEDGEMENTS

There are so many people to thank: Adam Thomas, Amy Glynn, Andrew McFadyen-Ketchum, Beth Adams, Brianna Pike, Carrie Jerrell, Chet Weise, Dale Ray Phillips, Dave Bonta, Heather Foster, Holly Goddard Jones, John Drury, Larry O. Dean, LaWanda Walters, Sally Brannen, Scott Woodham, Sean Singer, and Will Miller.

Special thanks to the faculty and staff of the Sewanee Writers' Conference—Mark Jarman (who was also my first real poetry teacher), Charles Martin, Cheri Bedell Peters, Wyatt Prunty, and especially the late Claudia Emerson, who read my manuscript and provided invaluable advice, both personal and poetic. Claudia, you are missed.

My immense surprise and gratitude go out to Jennifer Barber, who chose this manuscript for the Trio Award, as well as to Tayve Neese and Joanna Penn Cooper, my wonderful editors. Working with Trio Press has been an amazing experience.

Carrie Ann Baade provided the cover art for *Cleave*. I am still in awe, and my gratitude is boundless.

Gratitude beyond measure is also due to Sheila Sanderson, my first and best reader for over three decades; my children, Dan and Raleigh; my parents, Kenneth and Yvonne; and my grandmother, Elizabeth Blincoe, who first read Keats and Tennyson to me. "Shame at the Five and Dime" is for her.

My heroes have always been teachers, so it's most important to thank my own mentors: Daniel Anderson, Brian Barker, Nickole Brown, and Philip Stephens. Without your friendship, your guidance, and the touchstones of your own poetry, there wouldn't be a book.

All the love poems in *Cleave* are for Harvey Ellison Parker—friend, lover, husband, teacher, and the very embodiment of Song of Songs 5:16. This book is for you.

Grateful acknowledgement is also made to the editors of journals and anthologies where these poems first found homes, sometimes in slightly different forms.

Alligator Juniper: "Unslaked," "Victorian Ladies Once Read in the Dark by Tracing Raised Type on a Book's Pages"

American Poetry Journal: "Coda: out of"

Anti-: "Still Life with Wicker"

Best New Poets 2011: "Housewifery: An Annotation"

Blue Fifth Review: "Here Lies One: Remembering You Through Cavafy," "*In Ictu Oculi,*" "Ornithology: Wild Canaries," "My Name Once Meant Comb of Sweetness," "Unchained Melody: The Studio Version"

Broadsided: "Ulysses: *Uxoria*"

Centrifugal Eye: "First Person Plural, First Person Singular"

Iron Horse Literary Review: "Triage," "It Pays to Increase Your Word Power: *Diminuendo*"

New Madrid: "Breasts"

Ocho: Poets Who Tweet: "the sixties: age ten and what i wanted was"

Other Four-Letter Words: "Aubade: Thrift Store Sidewalk Sestina"

Parable Press: "Anything in the Thicket," "Taking a Walk with You"

Pebble Creek Review: "I Stand Here Ironing: A Fairy Tale"

Poets and Artists: "In the Laundry Room," Shame at the Five and Dime," "Something to Declare"

qarrtsiluni: "Cameo: Epithalamion," "No Place like Home: Kansas 1965," "Materials and Not Enough Time"

Right Hand Pointing: "Dendrochrondrology: A Definition"

Soundzine: "A Cappella"

Spaces: "Blind Contour Drawing," "Eminent Domain," "Here Lies," "Widdershins"

Utter: "Process Through Which My Beloved Becomes a Diamond"

A Walk Through the Memory Palace: "78 RPM"

Whale Sound: "First Anniversary: Reading Russian Literature"

ABOUT THE AUTHOR

Pamela Johnson Parker is the author of two chapbooks, *Other Four-Letter Words* and *A Walk Through the Memory Palace,* which won the Qaartsiluni Prize. Her poetry, flash fiction, and lyric essays have appeared in journals such as *Iron Horse Literary Review, American Poetry Journal, diode, Poets and Artists, Anomaly,* and *Gamut.* Parker's work has also been featured in the anthologies *Language Lessons: Volume 1, Poets on Painting, The Rivers Anthology,* and *Best New Poets 2011,* judged by D.A. Powell. She works in the Department of Art & Design at Murray State University, where she has also taught creative writing, contemporary poetry, and forms of fiction.

About the Artist

Carrie Ann Baade is known for her allegorical oil paintings. These painted parables combine remnants of Renaissance and Baroque imagery, creating surreal landscapes inhabited by exotic flora, fauna, and figures. As a contemporary painter, she returns to the relevant moments in art history in order to reclaim them, not merely as a quotation of a theme or an image, but also as the materiality of methods and techniques that ultimately create them.

Carrie was awarded the Florida Division of Cultural Affairs Individual Artist Fellowship in 2010, the Delaware Division of the Arts Fellowship for Established Artist in 2005, and was nominated for the prestigious United States Artist Fellowship in 2006 and the Joan Mitchell Grant in 2012. Her work has been exhibited in museums and galleries nationally and internationally.

As a native born Louisianan, Carrie has deep southern roots yet she has traveled and studied painting history and techniques around the world. She received her Masters in Painting from the University of Delaware and her BFA from the School of the Art Institute of Chicago, which included one year of study at the Florence Academy of Art in Italy. She currently lives and works in Tallahassee where she is an Associate Professor of Painting and Drawing at Florida State University.

Website: **carrieannbaade.com**

About the Book

Cleave was designed at Trio House Press through the collaboration of:

Joanna Penn Cooper, Lead Editor
Tayve Neese, Supporting Editor
Cover Artwork: Carrie Ann Baade
Lea C. Deschenes, Interior & Cover Design

The text is set in Adobe Caslon Pro.

The publication of this book is made possible, whole or in part,
by the generous support of the following individuals and/or agencies:

Anonymous

About the Press

Trio House Press is a collective press. Individuals within our organization come together and are motivated by the primary shared goal of publishing distinct American voices in poetry. All THP published poets must agree to serve as Collective Members of the Trio House Press for twenty-four months after publication in order to assist with the press and bring more Trio books into print. Award winners and published poets must serve on one of four committees: Production and Design, Distribution and Sales, Educational Development, or Fundraising and Marketing. Our Collective Members reside in cities from New York to San Francisco.

Trio House Press adheres to and supports all ethical standards and guidelines outlined by the CLMP.

Trio House Press, Inc. is dedicated to the promotion of poetry as literary art, which enhances the human experience and its culture. We contribute in an innovative and distinct way to American Poetry by publishing emerging and established poets, providing educational materials, and fostering the artistic process of writing poetry. For further information, or to consider making a donation to Trio House Press, please visit us online at: www.triohousepress.org.

Other Trio House Press Books you might enjoy:

Two Towns Over by Darren C. Demaree
      2017 Trio Award Winner selected by Campbell McGrath

Bird~Brain by Matt Mauch, 2017

Dark Tussock Moth by Mary Cisper
      2016 Trio Award Winner selected by Bhisham Bherwani

Break the Habit by Tara Betts, 2016

Bone Music by Stephen Cramer
      2015 Louise Bogan Award selected by Kimiko Hahn

*Rigging a Chevy into a Time Machine and Other Ways
      to Escape a Plague* by Carolyn Hembree
      2015 Trio Award Winner selected by Neil Shepard

Magpies in the Valley of Oleanders by Kyle McCord, 2015

Your Immaculate Heart by Annmarie O'Connell, 2015

The Alchemy of My Mortal Form by Sandy Longhorn
      2014 Louise Bogan Winner selected by Carol Frost

What the Night Numbered by Bradford Tice
    2014 Trio Award Winner selected by Peter Campion

Flight of August by Lawrence Eby
    2013 Louise Bogan Winner selected by Joan Houlihan

The Consolations by John W. Evans
    2013 Trio Award Winner selected by Mihaela Moscaliuc

Fellow Odd Fellow by Steven Riel, 2013

Clay by David Groff
    2012 Louise Bogan Winner selected by Michael Waters

Gold Passage by Iris Jamahl Dunkle
    2012 Trio Award Winner selected by Ross Gay

If You're Lucky Is a Theory of Mine by Matt Mauch, 2012

9 780996 586481